I0886062

ART & DESIGN CAREERS

A Career in FASHION DESIGN

Mitchell Lane PUBLISHERS

Nancy Coffelt

Mitchell Lane
PUBLISHERS

mitchelllanepub.com

2001 SW 31st Avenue
Hallandale, FL 33009

First Edition, 2026.
Author: Nancy Coffelt
Designer: Ed Morgan
Editor: Tammy Gagne

Series: Art and Design Careers
Title: A Career in Fashion Design

Library bound ISBN: 979-8-89260-500-7
eBook ISBN: 979-8-89260-510-6

Photo credits: cover, contents, 5, 7, 9, 13, 23, 31, 37, 41, 43 freepik.com; p. 15 wikimedia; p. 17, 21, 25, 29, 33, 35 Shutterstock; p. 19, 27 Alamy; p. 39 wikimedia

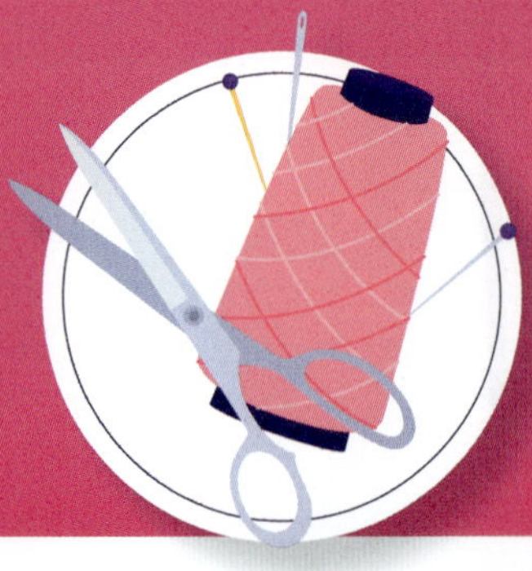

Contents

Chapter One

A Little Imagination

Toby followed her friend Charles into the resale shop. "I love **thrifting**," Charles said. He spotted a rack of shirts and was heading over to it.

"Me, too," Toby answered. Toby had just moved to Fairview. She hadn't made many new friends yet. She was grateful to have met Charles at school. He seemed to like clothes as much as she did. She found a rack of dresses. "Hmm," she said holding one up. The skirt was long and spotted with tiny daisies, suiting her perfectly. But the collar was too frilly, not her style at all.

"Are you going to get that?" Charles asked as he flipped through the shirts one rack over from her.

CHAPTER ONE

Toby hung the dress back up. "No," she replied. "The top is hideous." She held up another dress. This time she liked the top. The neckline was perfect. The skirt wasn't her taste, though. She grabbed the first dress and layered its bottom under the top of the other. She showed them to Charles. "I wish I could snap my fingers and combine these dresses."

"You totally could," Charles told her.

"What do you mean?" Toby was confused.

"Cut the top off that one and sew it onto the other," Charles suggested. He made it sound like it *was* as easy as snapping her fingers. He showed her the shirt he had over his arm. "The front of this is great," he said. But when he turned it around, she saw a stain across the back.

"That's too bad," Toby said.

"It's fixable," Charles said, "just like your dresses." His eyes got wide. "Almost forgot." He hurried to the back of the store. Toby trotted behind him, unsure of where he was headed. It didn't look like there were any clothes in this direction.

A Little Imagination

Thrift stores provide a variety of patterns and fabrics to choose from.

CHAPTER ONE

Charles stopped at a shelf stacked with blankets. He pulled out a fleece one and then a quilted one. Soon, he had collected six blankets in different textures, colors, and prints.

"How cold do you get?" Toby asked. She was even more confused now.

"They're for my sister," Charles laughed. "She uses them for her fashion projects. I told her I would find her some cool blankets."

"What kind of projects?" Toby asked as she stroked the soft fleece.

Charles reached for his smartphone. He did some scrolling and showed the screen to Toby. A girl in the video was making a sewing pattern. She placed it on top of a blanket before adding pins. She then cut and sewed the fabric. In the final frame, the blanket had been transformed into a tracksuit. "That's my sister," Charles said proudly. "She wants to be a fashion designer."

"Wow!" Toby was amazed. "Do you think she could help me with the dresses?"

Charles nodded. "I could, too. I'm thinking about studying fashion as well."

Preowned Sewing Machines

The newest and fanciest sewing machines can be expensive. But young people interested in fashion design can often find good deals on preowned models. Fabric stores, flea markets, and online marketplaces such as eBay can be great places to locate a gently used sewing machine at a fraction of the cost of a new item.

CHAPTER ONE

Charles showed her another video. This time, his sister transformed a dated dress into a trendy romper. Toby could hardly believe how different the garment looked at the end.

"I think this fabric would look great as the new back of the stained shirt," Charles said, pointing to the quilt. "What do you think?"

Toby suddenly saw the old blankets in a new light. The clothes on the racks also looked different to her now. None of the items had to stay the way it was. A little imagination could turn each one into something completely different.

"I'm buying the dresses," Toby told Charles. She had never thought of fashion design as something that young people like them could do. But she was excited to learn more.

A Little Imagination

Blankets can be used in place of new material for making clothes.

Chapter Two

From Idea to Hanger

Fashion designers are the artists behind the clothing styles people wear every day. Shirts, pants, suits, dresses, and shoes must be designed before they can be produced for sale. Designers begin by sketching their ideas. Then they turn the ideas into patterns so they can sew a **prototype** of each design. Once a new design has been approved, a manufacturer can produce the item as part of a new clothing collection. All the clothing seen on fashion runways and in clothing stores follows this process. Fashion designers can set trends, address needs, highlight culture, and even help the environment.

CHAPTER TWO

In the 1860s, dressmaker Charles Frederick Worth was enjoying great success. Napoleon III was a European military leader who crowned himself France's emperor in 1804. His wife, Empress Eugenie, helped Worth become successful. The Empress wanted him to design clothes that fit her lavish sense of style. When other people in France's upper class saw his designs, they wanted him to design clothes for them as well. Worth is often called the father of *haute couture*. In French, this phrase means "high sewing" or "high dressmaking." Today, people use the term to describe clothing created by the top designers.

By 1989, Vera Wang had already begun her career in fashion. She'd been an editor at *Vogue* magazine, which focuses on fashion trends. She'd also designed **accessories** for designer Ralph Lauren. When she was thirty-nine, a search for her own wedding dress changed Wang's career. "I looked everywhere, from department stores to Chanel couture," she told *Harvard Business Review*. When she had no luck, her father suggested that she see the situation as an opportunity to design bridal wear.

From Idea to Hanger

Empress Eugenie influenced styles worn by the wealthy in early nineteenth-century France.

CHAPTER TWO

Wang sees her background as vital to her success. "Start by working for somebody you respect—or anybody, really—and get paid to learn. If you don't educate yourself first, you really can't break rules." Wang's designs have been embraced by numerous celebrities. Her clients include Mariah Carey, Ariana Grande, and Kim and Khloe Kardashian.

Kenneth Ize was born in Lagos, Nigeria, and raised in Austria. He started his design house in 2013. Ize has always loved clothes. "There's nothing like when I'm wearing something that makes me feel one thousand and one percent myself," he told *The Talks* website. "If I feel amazing wearing something, it gives me power."

From Idea to Hanger

Vera Wang manufactures most of her bridal collections in the United States.

CHAPTER TWO

Ize studied fashion and design at the University of Applied Arts Vienna and is known for simple silhouettes. A silhouette is the outline or shape of a garment when it is being worn. His collections are usually unisex, which means the clothes are designed for either men or women. Based in Nigeria, Kenneth Ize's design house employs thirty traditional weavers. It is the biggest weaving factory in the African nation. Ize also uses recycled items in his work. For his 2023 collection, he used old T-shirts that were bleached and dyed. He stitched them over pre-owned jeans. This technique from northern Nigeria is called *ise owo*. In English, this means "work done with the hand."

From Idea to Hanger

Kenneth Ize uses striped patterns in many of his designs.

CHAPTER TWO

Kuwaiti-born Nadine Mosallam designs for multiple body types. Her clothing is meant to hug the body. "Literally anyone can wear it, and it still looks good," Mosallam told *Vogue*. Mosallam uses deadstock in her designs. This is leftover fabric or scraps from factories. It often comes from pieces of clothing that never sold, which Mosallam sees as useful fabric. "Everything's very **sustainable** . . . and I use **vintage** and deadstock material. Once a piece is sold out, that's it. It's on to the next collection."

Reducing, Reusing, and Recycling

The production of clothing fibers, such as cotton and wool, is predicted to grow to 147 million tons by 2030. Most of this material, as much as 85 percent, goes into landfills when clothing is outgrown or no longer wanted. This is about one garbage truck full of clothes being dumped or **incinerated** every second. Using materials that might end up in a landfill, such as deadstock, is a practical way to reduce this waste.

Chapter
Three

Design Meets Technology

Fashion designers use imagination to create their designs. But they need art skills to sketch those designs. Art education helps designers understand how the colors and patterns of fabric work together. Designers must also have sewing skills to produce prototypes based on their sketches. Computer software, such as Adobe Illustrator, can be helpful during this process.

Design software assists in the patternmaking process by creating a two-dimensional image of a design. That image later turns into the clothing pattern. The program helps the designer easily reproduce the pattern in different sizes. Design software helps speed up the production of a clothing line. And it also helps reduce human errors.

CHAPTER THREE

Brad Lacey is a shoe designer for New Balance footwear. He views design software as a way of pushing both creativity and production. "When we all started designing in Adobe Illustrator, for example, we could already see that the way we designed sneakers had evolved. We could be hyper accurate, enlarge the image, and so on. You saw sneakers change," he told Heuritech, a company that predicts business trends in the fashion industry. "Designers aren't trying to solve a problem that hasn't already been solved; rather, they're spending their time on more forward thinking."

Fashion designers also need effective communication skills. Designers work with many other people, such as assistant designers and interns. A fashion design intern is a person learning the industry by observing and helping with the design and production process. Designers must express their vision to these assistants. Designers also work with manufacturers, fashion editors, members of the press, and retail buyers. They must have good listening skills and accept feedback.

Design Meets Technology

Sneakers have evolved from simple sportswear to fashion statements.

CHAPTER THREE

Even before entering a college fashion design program or internship, there are many steps hopeful fashion designers can take. Signing up for art, sewing, and computer classes can provide a great start. Often, shops that sell sewing machines offer classes. School career counselors may know about additional computer training classes in a particular community.

Developing an eye for fashion is a must for anyone interested in this ever-changing field. One way to do this is by following fashion designers on social media. Most libraries subscribe to fashion magazines, providing another way for young people to stay up to date on trends. In this type of magazine, the ads can be just as important as the articles. The ads are promoting the latest offerings from some of the most successful fashion designers.

Changing the Direction of Fashion

Social media has provided a place for lesser-known fashion designers to showcase their work. These posts have led to more than just sales for new designers. Social media posts have also become part of trendsetting. Posting to apps such as Instagram and Snapchat can spread designs to millions of people across the globe in just seconds. Inspired by the 2023 movie *Barbie*, many young fashion designers made Barbiecore one of the top design trends for 2024. This was the name given to the feminine pink clothing style for which the popular doll of the same name is known.

Business skills are also a must for anyone planning to enter the fashion design industry. Many high schools and colleges offer business classes. Taking some of these courses will also help prepare a student for the fashion design industry. Young people can also learn about fashion sales by getting a part-time or summer job at a retail clothing store.

Designer Marc Jacobs stresses the importance of learning the basics. He learned to sew his own clothes at an early age. It helped him understand how fabric affected his designs. He encourages young designers to experiment with sewing. "Run some fabric through a sewing machine. Change the stitch. Change the tension of the stitch, and see what it does," Jacobs says in his MasterClass.

Pay attention to details and look around for inspiration. Carry a notebook. Watch what people are wearing. Jacobs says that inspiration is everywhere. "I always think for fashion to have a life, it needs to come from life," Jacobs says. "I keep my eyes open when I'm on the street or when I'm in a car and looking out the window. I think life is inspiring."

Design Meets Technology

Marc Jacobs was creative director for Louis Vuitton for sixteen years.

Chapter Four

Preparing for a Show

Once a designer has produced a collection of clothing designs, it's time to introduce the fashions to consumers. An effective way to do this is to take part in a fashion show. Before the audience can applaud for the designs, though, a lot of work must happen backstage. Designers must make sure the clothing fits each model perfectly. This often means ironing the fabric and making last-minute **alterations**. Hair and makeup teams make the models look their best. Designers also add accessories, such as jewelry and handbags, to complete the outfits. Once the designer gives the final approval, the models can start strutting down the catwalk. This is the raised, narrow platform where models walk during a show.

CHAPTER FOUR

In 2023, designer Kate Roberts faced some challenges at her first show during the New York Fashion Week event. Three of her models didn't show up. Pieces in her collection needed alterations. Roberts told the *Fashion Mingle* website that overseeing the production of her collection "required **flexibility** and staying on my toes." She also said she couldn't have done it on her own. She relied on the help of stylist Jes Ruzic. "I couldn't have done the show without her."

The runway isn't the only place designers can showcase their work. Trade shows feature many designer booths. There, buyers for clothing stores can see numerous offerings all in the same place.

Pop-up shops are stores that set up and operate for short periods, usually just days or weeks. In these settings, designers can sell their work without having to rent a space for a longer time. Designer Bishme R. Cromartie uses pop-up shops to better connect with his clients. "Pop-up shops are like mini presentations. I get a chance to showcase the garments up close and personal with familiar and new clients," he told the *E D G E Fashion Intelligence* website. "I find it great because they are able to ask me questions about my inspiration behind the garments."

Fashion Week

Fashion Week is a collection of parties and runway shows that are held twice a year. Summer collections are introduced in September, and winter collections are shown in March. This gives manufacturers time to produce the designs for retail. There are more than one hundred Fashion Weeks worldwide. The largest and most popular ones are held in New York, Paris, London, and Milan.

Trunk shows are events where designers show their work at an existing store or boutique. They are usually no more than a few hours long. Like pop-up shops, trunk shows let designers connect directly with clients. They allow designers to take orders and ship pieces to clients once the items are completed. Herbert Victoria likes the opportunity to personally engage with his customers through trunk shows. He says they have also brought him financial success. "I've made more money doing trunk shows than anywhere else, and plan on [continuing] that way until I find most of my clothes in stores," he told the *E D G E Fashion Intelligence* website.

Lookbooks are catalogs of design photoshoots. They show a designer's work on models. Lookbooks are designed carefully to attract the attention of clients, retail buyers, and the media. The photos are usually also posted on a designer's website. Designers send out emails to potential buyers directing them to their websites as new items are featured. To further market their lookbooks, designers may also print and mail parts of them as ads for their new clothing.

Preparing for a Show

Makeup artists and photographers play important roles in introducing a new clothing collection.

Chapter
Five

Designing a Future

There have been many famous fashion designers who didn't graduate from a fashion design program. What most designers have in common is their background in design. Giorgio Armani once worked as a window dresser, arranging merchandise for a department store in Milan. Pierre Cardin studied **architecture**. At age fourteen, Karl Lagerfeld entered a coat design contest in Paris and won.

While a formal education isn't necessary, there are benefits to attending a fashion design program. Young people interested in fashion may have many ideas. But they may not know where to start in turning them into designs. A fashion program teaches students the basics of garment design and construction. The courses also expose students to a variety of design experiences and approaches.

A fashion program can also offer opportunities in the industry, such as internships, **grants**, and access to industrial tools such as knitting machines. Many programs provide computer labs with the latest design software. Parsons School of Design in New York offers a Bachelor of Fine Arts program. It balances handwork such as sewing with digital design. The school also has students work with established companies such as Saks Fifth Avenue, Louis Vuitton, Swarovski, and Coach.

Ben Barry is the dean at Parsons's School of Fashion. In an interview with Studio Art Quilt Associates, he explained why he believes a fashion program is important for students. "Design education can transform current thinking and practices because it shapes the world views and processes of the next generation of makers and designers."

Designing a Future

Parsons School of Design was used as the stage for the reality show *Project Runway*.

CHAPTER FIVE

Designer Betsey Johnson first studied art at the Pratt Institute in New York. She went on to study fabric design at Syracuse University in New York. Johnson credits her education for her success. "I selected my college because [I] thought I would be an artist or commercial **illustrator**; I never thought I'd be a designer. There is an advantage to attend design school because you'll learn the history of fashion, draping, sewing, and cutting, but I got more out of art school [than I would have] out of fashion school because I could already cut and sew. It boils down to a lot of hard work and really loving what you do."

Other Jobs in Fashion

Many jobs are available in the fashion industry. Trend forecasters research the market and identify colors, fabrics, and styles that may soon become popular. These findings can help designers know what may sell best. Creative directors oversee design teams and plan advertising campaigns. Fashion buyers find and purchase the materials needed for a line, such as fabrics.

CHAPTER FIVE

Students who cannot afford the cost of a fashion program can apply for scholarships. These financial awards are granted to students to help pay for further education. The Thea Foundation Fashion Design Competition offers one of these awards. The competition is open to all high school seniors in the state of Arkansas. Judges consider entries of clothing, accessories, and costumes. The top three winners receive up to $10,000 in scholarship funds. The Taiwan Fashion Design Award also offers a top prize of $10,000. This scholarship focuses on designs that feature creativity, practicality, and sustainability. Finalists also get free travel to a runway show in Taiwan.

A career in this field may begin with a passion for designing clothes. But it can grow into a bigger goal, such as changing trends, expanding fashion options for overlooked customers, or even helping to reduce waste on the planet. There's no telling what the next generation of fashion designers might accomplish.

Designing a Future

Turning ideas into designs, one stitch at a time

Glossary

accessories
Items such as jewelry or handbags that complete an outfit

alterations
Changes made to a completed garment to make it fit someone better

architecture
The art of designing buildings and other large structures

flexibility
The ability to adapt to changing needs

grants
Gifts of money marked for a particular purpose

incinerated
Disposed of by burning to ashes

illustrator
A person who creates drawings for publications such as books or magazines

prototype
A piece of clothing used as an early example of a design

sustainable
Able to use supplies without endangering resources

thrifting
Shopping for good deals on preowned items

vintage
From a previous period but of enduring interest

Ready, Set, Design!

Test your new knowledge of fashion design by answering the following questions.

1. **Vera Wang began her fashion career designing accessories for:**
   - **A.** Ralph Lauren
   - **B.** Charles Frederick Worth
   - **C.** Kenneth Ize
2. **A fashion design intern is someone who:**
   - **A.** Teaches by demonstrating
   - **B.** Learns by observing
   - **C.** Designs a clothing line
3. **What do lookbooks feature?**
   - **A.** Sketches of possible designs
   - **B.** Patterns of designs to be sewn
   - **C.** Photos of designs on models
4. **What does Betsey Johnson credit for her success in fashion design?**
   - **A.** Her education
   - **B.** Trunk shows
   - **C.** An internship

Answers: A, B, C, A

Find Out More

IN PRINT

Bithell, Rachel. *A Career in Illustration*. Mitchell Lane Publishers, 2026.

Huwiler, Madeleine. *Fashion Design School for Kids and Teens*. Bye Bye Studio, 2023.

Quigley, Kerri. *Fashion Design for Kids*. Callisto Publishing, 2021.

ON THE INTERNET

Drew, Mikelle. "So Why Should You Go to Fashion School?" *383 Design Studio*, May 20, 2023.
www.383designstudionyc.com/post/so-why-should-you-go-to-fashion-school

"Fashion Designer," *Career Girls*, n.d.
www.careergirls.org/careers/fashion-designer

"Inside the Fashion Design Process from Briefs to Assembly," *MasterClass*, June 7, 2021.
www.masterclass.com/articles/inside-the-fashion-design-process-from-briefs-to-assemblystudents

Index

About the Author

Nancy Coffelt's mother taught her how to sew. Coffelt enjoyed making her own clothes in high school. She still enjoys creating fashion, focusing on visible mending, a decorative way to mend worn spots in clothing.